The Month Of: 1 2 3 4 5 6 7 8 9 10 11 12

SUNDAY	MONDAY	TUESDAY	WEDNESDAY
○	○	○	○
○	○	○	○
○	○	○	○
○	○	○	○
○	○	○	○

THURSDAY	FRIDAY	SATURDAY	NOTES
○	○	○	
○	○	○	
○	○	○	
○	○	○	
○	○	○	

The Week Of: /   /

MONDAY	TUESDAY

THURSDAY	FRIDAY

WEDNESDAY	GOALS OF THE WEEK
SATURDAY/SUNDAY	NOTES

The Week Of: /   /

MONDAY

TUESDAY

THURSDAY

FRIDAY

WEDNESDAY

GOALS OF THE WEEK

SATURDAY/SUNDAY

NOTES

The Week Of: /   /

MONDAY	TUESDAY
THURSDAY	FRIDAY

WEDNESDAY	GOALS OF THE WEEK

SATURDAY/SUNDAY	NOTES

The Week Of: /   /

MONDAY	TUESDAY

THURSDAY	FRIDAY

WEDNESDAY

GOALS OF THE WEEK

SATURDAY/SUNDAY

NOTES

The Week Of: /   /

MONDAY

TUESDAY

THURSDAY

FRIDAY

WEDNESDAY

GOALS OF THE WEEK

SATURDAY/SUNDAY

NOTES

The Month Of: 1 2 3 4 5 6 7 8 9 10 11 12

SUNDAY	MONDAY	TUESDAY	WEDNESDAY
○	○	○	○
○	○	○	○
○	○	○	○
○	○	○	○
○	○	○	○

THURSDAY	FRIDAY	SATURDAY	NOTES
○	○	○	
○	○	○	
○	○	○	
○	○	○	
○	○	○	

The Week Of: /   /

MONDAY	TUESDAY

THURSDAY	FRIDAY

WEDNESDAY	GOALS OF THE WEEK
SATURDAY/SUNDAY	NOTES

The Week Of: /   /

MONDAY	TUESDAY

THURSDAY	FRIDAY

WEDNESDAY	GOALS OF THE WEEK
SATURDAY/SUNDAY	NOTES

The Week Of: /   /

MONDAY	TUESDAY

THURSDAY	FRIDAY

WEDNESDAY	GOALS OF THE WEEK
SATURDAY/SUNDAY	NOTES

The Week Of: __ / __ / __

MONDAY

TUESDAY

THURSDAY

FRIDAY

WEDNESDAY	GOALS OF THE WEEK
SATURDAY/SUNDAY	NOTES

The Week Of: /   /

MONDAY	TUESDAY

THURSDAY	FRIDAY

WEDNESDAY

GOALS OF THE WEEK

SATURDAY/SUNDAY

NOTES

"As long as I'm Alive, I know tha

"I'm gonna live!"

THE SOUTHERN SUN

The Month Of: 1 2 3 4 5 6 7 8 9 10 11 12

SUNDAY	MONDAY	TUESDAY	WEDNESDAY
○	○	○	○
○	○	○	○
○	○	○	○
○	○	○	○
○	○	○	○

THURSDAY	FRIDAY	SATURDAY	NOTES
○	○	○	
○	○	○	
○	○	○	
○	○	○	
○	○	○	

The Week Of: /   /

MONDAY	TUESDAY

THURSDAY	FRIDAY

WEDNESDAY	GOALS OF THE WEEK
SATURDAY/SUNDAY	NOTES

The Week Of: /   /

MONDAY	TUESDAY

THURSDAY	FRIDAY

WEDNESDAY

GOALS OF THE WEEK

SATURDAY/SUNDAY

NOTES

The Week Of: /   /

MONDAY	TUESDAY

THURSDAY	FRIDAY

WEDNESDAY	GOALS OF THE WEEK

SATURDAY/SUNDAY	NOTES
	_____
	_____
	_____
	_____
	_____

The Week Of: /   /

MONDAY	TUESDAY

THURSDAY	FRIDAY

WEDNESDAY	GOALS OF THE WEEK
SATURDAY/SUNDAY	NOTES

The Week Of: /   /

MONDAY	TUESDAY

THURSDAY	FRIDAY

WEDNESDAY

GOALS OF THE WEEK

SATURDAY/SUNDAY

NOTES

The Month Of: 1 2 3 4 5 6 7 8 9 10 11 12

SUNDAY	MONDAY	TUESDAY	WEDNESDAY
○	○	○	○
○	○	○	○
○	○	○	○
○	○	○	○
○	○	○	○

THURSDAY	FRIDAY	SATURDAY	NOTES
○	○	○	
○	○	○	
○	○	○	
○	○	○	
○	○	○	

The Week Of: /   /

MONDAY	TUESDAY

THURSDAY	FRIDAY

WEDNESDAY	GOALS OF THE WEEK

SATURDAY/SUNDAY	NOTES

The Week Of: /   /

MONDAY	TUESDAY

THURSDAY	FRIDAY

WEDNESDAY	GOALS OF THE WEEK

SATURDAY/SUNDAY	NOTES

The Week Of: /   /

MONDAY	TUESDAY

THURSDAY	FRIDAY

WEDNESDAY	GOALS OF THE WEEK

SATURDAY/SUNDAY	NOTES

The Week Of: /   /

MONDAY

TUESDAY

THURSDAY

FRIDAY

WEDNESDAY	GOALS OF THE WEEK

SATURDAY/SUNDAY	NOTES

The Week Of: /   /

MONDAY	TUESDAY

THURSDAY	FRIDAY

WEDNESDAY	GOALS OF THE WEEK
SATURDAY/SUNDAY	NOTES

The Month Of: 1 2 3 4 5 6 7 8 9 10 11 12

SUNDAY	MONDAY	TUESDAY	WEDNESDAY
○	○	○	○
○	○	○	○
○	○	○	○
○	○	○	○
○	○	○	○

THURSDAY	FRIDAY	SATURDAY	NOTES
○	○	○	
○	○	○	
○	○	○	
○	○	○	
○	○	○	

The Week Of: /   /

MONDAY	TUESDAY

THURSDAY	FRIDAY

WEDNESDAY	GOALS OF THE WEEK
SATURDAY/SUNDAY	NOTES

The Week Of: /   /

MONDAY

TUESDAY

THURSDAY

FRIDAY

WEDNESDAY	GOALS OF THE WEEK
SATURDAY/SUNDAY	NOTES

The Week Of: /   /

MONDAY

TUESDAY

THURSDAY

FRIDAY

WEDNESDAY	GOALS OF THE WEEK

SATURDAY/SUNDAY	NOTES

The Week Of: /   /

MONDAY

TUESDAY

THURSDAY

FRIDAY

WEDNESDAY	GOALS OF THE WEEK
SATURDAY/SUNDAY	NOTES

The Week Of: /   /

MONDAY	TUESDAY

THURSDAY	FRIDAY

WEDNESDAY	GOALS OF THE WEEK

SATURDAY/SUNDAY	NOTES

The Month Of: 1 2 3 4 5 6 7 8 9 10 11 12

SUNDAY	MONDAY	TUESDAY	WEDNESDAY
○	○	○	○
○	○	○	○
○	○	○	○
○	○	○	○
○	○	○	○

THURSDAY	FRIDAY	SATURDAY	NOTES
○	○	○	
○	○	○	
○	○	○	
○	○	○	
○	○	○	

The Week Of: /   /

MONDAY	TUESDAY

THURSDAY	FRIDAY

WEDNESDAY	GOALS OF THE WEEK

SATURDAY/SUNDAY	NOTES

The Week Of: /   /

MONDAY	TUESDAY

THURSDAY	FRIDAY

WEDNESDAY	GOALS OF THE WEEK

SATURDAY/SUNDAY	NOTES

The Week Of: /   /

MONDAY

TUESDAY

THURSDAY

FRIDAY

WEDNESDAY	**GOALS OF THE WEEK**
SATURDAY/SUNDAY	**NOTES**

The Week Of: /   /

MONDAY	TUESDAY

THURSDAY	FRIDAY

WEDNESDAY	GOALS OF THE WEEK

SATURDAY/SUNDAY	NOTES

The Week Of: /   /

MONDAY	TUESDAY

THURSDAY	FRIDAY

WEDNESDAY	GOALS OF THE WEEK

SATURDAY/SUNDAY	NOTES

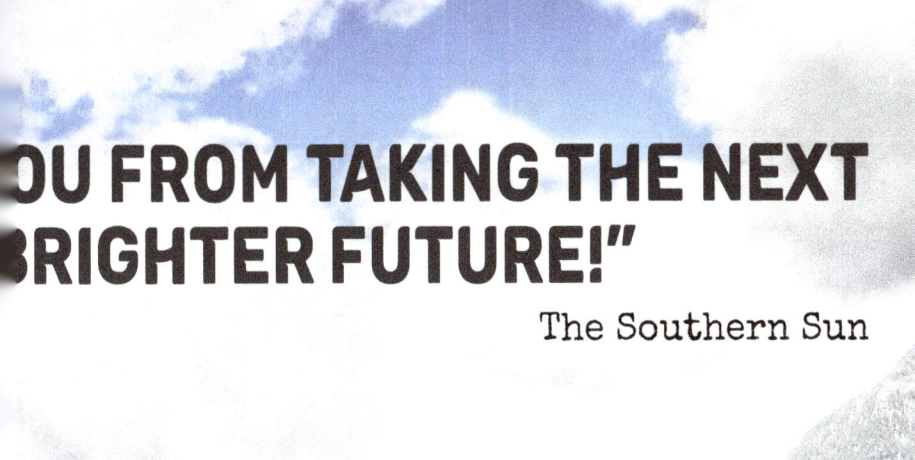

OU FROM TAKING THE NEXT
RIGHTER FUTURE!"

The Southern Sun

LIST & THINGS TO REMEMBER

LIST & THINGS TO REMEMBER

LIST & THINGS TO REMEMBER

LIST & THINGS TO REMEMBER

LIST & THINGS TO REMEMBER

LIST & THINGS TO REMEMBER

LIST & THINGS TO REMEMBER

LIST & THINGS TO REMEMBER

LIST & THINGS TO REMEMBER

LIST & THINGS TO REMEMBER

www.ingramcontent.com/pod-product-compliance
Lightning Source LLC
Chambersburg PA
CBHW071146060526
44107CB00133B/333